EDGE BOOKS

HALLOWEEN EXTREME

HOW TO BUILD

Hair-Raising

HAUNTED HOUSES

by Megan Cooley Peterson

CAPSTONE PRESS
a capstone imprint

Edge Books are published by Capstone Press,
151 Good Counsel Drive, P.O. Box 669, Mankato, Minnesota 56002.
www.capstonepub.com

Books published by Capstone Press are manufactured with paper
containing at least 10 percent post-consumer waste.

Library of Congress Cataloging-in-Publication Data
Peterson, Megan Cooley.
  How to build hair-raising haunted houses / by Megan Cooley Peterson.
     p. cm.—(Edge books. halloween extreme)
  Includes bibliographical references and index.
  Summary: "Provides step-by-step instructions for building haunted houses using
household materials"—Provided by publisher.
  ISBN 978-1-4296-5421-0 (library binding)
  1. Haunted houses (Amusements) 2. Halloween decorations—Juvenile literature.
I. Peterson, Megan Cooley. II. Title. III. Series.
TT900.H32P44 2011
745.594'1646—dc22   2010030174

Editorial Credits

Shelly Lyons, editor; Tracy Davies, designer; Sarah Schuette, photo stylist;
    Marcy Morin, project production; Eric Manske, production specialist

APR 1 1 2011

Photo credits:

All photos by Capstone Studio/Karon Dubke

Artistic Effects

Shutterstock/aispl, Merkushev Vasiliy, Marafona, Paul B. Moore, Potapov
Alexander, Randall Mikulas, Renee Reeder BFA, Steven Bourelle

Printed in the United States of America in Stevens Point, Wisconsin.
092010   005934WZS11

Table of Contents

Introduction

It's Halloween night, and you're out trick-or-treating with your friends. A chill runs up your back as you pass by the creepiest house in the neighborhood. Paint peels from the siding. Shutters hang crookedly from broken windows. Your friends are too afraid to ring the doorbell. But you bravely approach the front door, hoping to get a piece of candy—and a peak inside.

Have you always wanted to create the spookiest haunted house on the block? You'll find plenty of creepy and gross ideas inside this book! And the best part is that you can find most of the supplies you'll need in your own home. Use dead leaves, newspaper, garbage bags, and even old bedsheets to create a fun house filled with **sinister** surprises.

Are you ready to build a hair-raising haunted house? Let's get started!

Decking out your house for Halloween is fun. But be sure to keep safety in mind. Ask an adult for help when hanging your ghoulish creations from ceilings and high tree branches. Also ask an adult to help you work with dangerous items such as a pumpkin carving saw tool and dry ice. Dry ice can burn your skin.

Tools

duct tape

pumpkin carving scraping tool

pumpkin carving saw tool

sinister—seeming evil and threatening

Lawn of the Dead

Before guests enter your house of horrors, spook them with a front lawn full of lost souls. Turn garbage bags into eerie ghosts. Top off the project with a flying ghost, and wait for the screaming to begin.

WHAT YOU NEED:

white bedsheet,
   twin size
scissors
1 wire clothes hanger
old newspaper or leaves
white yarn
masking tape
rope
fishing line
white plastic
   garbage bags
black construction paper
paintbrush
green glow-in-the-dark
   acrylic paint
double-sided tape

FLYING GHOST

Step 1: To find the center, fold the bedsheet in half. Then fold it in half again. Using the scissors, make a cut where all the folds are joined. Spread out the sheet.

Step 2: Bend down the sides of a wire hanger. Insert the hook of the hanger through the hole in the sheet.

Step 3: To create the ghost's head, place plenty of newspaper around the hanger. Gather the sheet around the head and tie off with a few pieces of white yarn.

Step 4: Place small pieces of masking tape around the top of the sheet where the hanger sticks out. The tape will keep the sheet from tearing or fraying.

Step 5: Have an adult help you tie a rope between two trees or posts. Be sure the rope is out of the way so people don't accidentally walk into it.

Step 6: Tie a long piece of fishing line to the ghost's head. Then hang the ghost at one end of the rope. Bend the hanger around the rope to secure.

Step 7 (not pictured): When people walk by your house, slowly pull the ghost toward you. Be sure to hide so no one can see you.

PLASTIC GHOST

Step 1: Fill the bottom quarter of a white plastic garbage bag with leaves or old newspaper. Tie off the head with white yarn. If the bag has drawstrings, cut off the bottom edge and discard.

Step 2: Using a scissors, cut out two oval eyes and a round mouth from the black construction paper. Place a strip of double-sided tape on the back of each piece. Stick the eyes and mouth to the ghost's face. Paint with glow-in-the-dark paint. Let dry.

Step 3: Poke two small holes through the top of the ghost's head with the scissors. The holes should be about 1 inch (2.5 centimeters) apart. Thread fishing line through the holes to act as a hanger. Repeat steps 1–3 for each ghost you make.

Step 4: Have an adult help you hang the ghosts from tree branches or posts on your front porch. You can also set ghosts in bushes and on the ground.

TIP

Do you have a fishing pole? Use it to reel in your flying ghost.

Man in the Window

Nothing screams a haunted house like a **silhouette** of someone who is trying to escape. Using cardboard and an old bedsheet, you can turn an ordinary window into a terrifying nightmare. Your friends will shake with fear as they knock on your front door.

WHAT YOU NEED:

marker
large piece of cardboard
scissors
old newspaper
black spray paint
fishing line
masking tape
white bedsheet, large
    enough to
    cover window
large suction cup
    with hook
small desk lamp
chair

silhouette—an outline of something that shows its shape

Step 1: On a piece of cardboard, draw an outline of a man from the waist up with his hands above his head. Cut out with a scissors.

Step 2: Set the cardboard figure outside on old newspaper and spray paint it. Be sure to follow the instructions and safety precautions on the spray paint can. Let dry.

Step 3: Using the scissors, poke a small hole through the top of the man's head. Thread a piece of fishing line through the hole and tie.

Step 4: Using masking tape, attach the sheet to the window's frame. Secure the suction cup above the window.

Step 5: Hang the cutout on the suction cup hook. The painted side should face the sheet.

Step 6: Set a desk lamp on a chair a few feet away from the window. Turn on the lamp, and aim the light toward the cutout. Make sure the rest of the room is dark.

1

2

3

4

5

6

TIP

If you don't have cardboard, create the man using felt, construction paper, or poster board. Tape or glue the man onto the sheet.

Dracula's Coffin

Poor Count Dracula. It looks like a vampire hunter finally caught up with him. Turn your bathroom into the scene of the crime. Your friends will be relieved that the famous bloodsucker is dead. Or is he?

WHAT YOU NEED:
black marker
large piece of cardboard
scissors
old newspaper
brown spray paint
black cloth, large enough
    to cover the tub
masking tape
handful of dirt
brown , black, and white
    construction paper
clear tape
paintbrush
red acrylic paint
socks
glass jars with lids
water
red food coloring
wooden spoon
plastic fangs
red lightbulbs

Step 1: Draw Dracula's coffin shape on a large piece of cardboard. Cut out with scissors.

Step 2: Set the cardboard outside on old newspaper and spray paint it. Be sure to follow the instructions and safety precautions on the spray paint can. Let dry.

Step 3: Using a black marker, write the words "Dracula's Comfy Coffin" on the cardboard.

Step 4: Drape the tub in a black cloth. Lay the cardboard over the bathtub. Use masking tape to secure if needed. Sprinkle a little dirt on top of the coffin.

Step 5: To make the stake, roll brown construction paper into a cone. Secure with clear tape. Crumple it a little with your hands. Then paint the tip red and set on top of the coffin.

TIP

If your bathroom doesn't have a bathtub, lean your coffin lid up in one corner of the shower stall.

14

Step 6: To make Dracula's feet, stuff a pair of socks with old newspaper. Set the feet between the bottom end of the tub and the coffin. The feet should look like they're sticking out of the coffin.

Step 7: Fill the jars with water. Add two or three drops of red food coloring and stir. Drop plastic fangs into each jar. Then place the lids on the jars and set them around the tub.

Step 8: Cover your palm with red paint and press onto a few pieces of white construction paper. Let dry. Then cut out the hand shapes and tape to the tub walls with clear tape.

Step 9: Cut out bat shapes from the black construction paper. Tape to the walls with clear tape.

Step 10: Have an adult replace the regular lightbulbs with red lightbulbs. Be sure the room has enough light so your guests can find their way around.

Hairy Hallway

What's creepier than walking through spiderwebs? Finding your way through a dark hallway filled with webs and killer spiders!

WHAT YOU NEED:
scissors
black yarn
black streamers
painter's tape
blue lightbulb
black chenille stems,
   cut in half
paintbrush
glow-in-the-dark
   acrylic paint

Step 1: Cut long pieces of black yarn and streamers. Cut as many pieces as needed to fill the hallway. Cut the bottom ends of the streamers to look like fringe. Make sure the pieces are long enough to brush past your guests' shoulders.

Step 2: Have an adult tape the yarn and streamers to the ceiling. Then have an adult replace the regular lightbulb with a blue lightbulb.

Step 3: Cut four chenille stems in half. Twist the pieces together to make each spider. Bend the legs so they curl out from the spider's center. Create as many spiders as you would like. Tape them to the walls. Tie a few spiders to the yarn that's hanging from the ceiling.

Step 4: Paint several pairs of glow-in-the-dark dots on the streamers. The glowing dots will look like spider eyes.

TIP

Sprinkle popcorn on the floor in the hallway. Cover with garbage bags and tape down. Tell your friends the crunchy feeling under their feet is dead cockroaches!

The Dying Room

Turn your kitchen into a hospital with a crazy surgeon in charge. Ask a friend to play the "patient" while you play the "surgeon." Dare your visitors to touch the patient's guts. If the open cuts on your patient don't gross out your friends, the jars of spare body parts will!

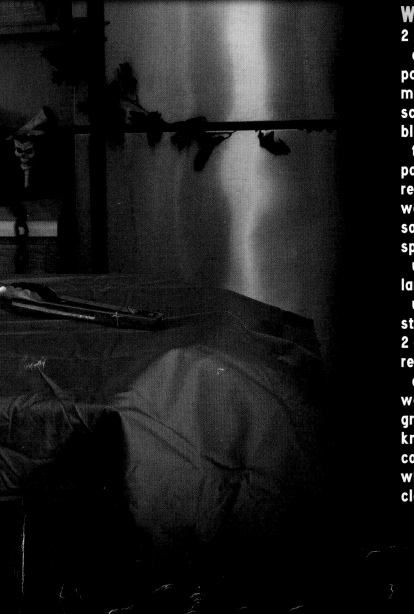

WHAT YOU NEED:

2 plastic sandwich
   containers
poster board
markers
scissors
blue fabric, large enough
   to drape over a table
paintbrush
red acrylic paint
water
saucepan
spaghetti noodles,
   uncooked
large shell noodles,
   uncooked
strainer
2 glass jars with lids
red and green food
   coloring
wooden spoon
green olives
knife
cauliflower
white construction paper
clear tape

Step 1: Set plastic sandwich containers on the center of a piece of poster board. Trace around them with a marker. Cut out the pieces with a scissors.

Step 2: Set the poster board on the middle of the fabric near the top edge. Trace the holes in the poster board onto the fabric. Make the holes in the fabric slightly smaller than the holes in the poster board. Cut out with scissors. Add red paint to the fabric to look like blood. Let dry.

Step 3: Have an adult help you boil water in a saucepan. Cook enough spaghetti and shell noodles to fill each sandwich container. Strain the noodles. Place the spaghetti noodles in one sandwich container and the shell noodles in the other container. Set aside.

Step 4: Fill the glass jars with water. Add six drops of red food coloring to one jar and stir. Drop in as many green olives as you'd like and add the lid. The olives will look like rotting eyeballs.

Step 5: Add six drops of green food coloring to the second jar and stir. Have an adult cut cauliflower to look like small brains. Insert the cauliflower and add the lid. Use markers and construction paper to make labels for the jars. Tape to the jars.

Step 6: Have your "patient" lie down on the kitchen table. Place the cardboard on top of the patient's torso. Set the plastic containers in the holes you cut.

Step 7: Drape the blue fabric over the patient's body. Make sure to line up the holes in the fabric with the plastic containers. Use clear tape to secure the fabric to the containers if needed.

Step 8: Set the jars of "spare parts" on a nearby counter or shelf. Make a sign telling guests what they are.

Step 9: Write the words "Cut 'Em Up Hospital: Enter If You Dare" on a piece of construction paper. Tape the sign to a wall or other surface.

TIP

Cut apart large black garbage bags and tape them to the walls. The bags will help make your haunted house look dark and spooky.

21

Faces in the Fog

Use dry ice, paper plates, and old sheets to create a room filled with spooks. Tell your friends the crazy surgeon's former "patients" are now haunting the living room.

WHAT YOU NEED:

old white bedsheets
thumbtacks
masking tape
paintbrush
glow-in-the-dark
    acrylic paint
white paper plates
cheesecloth
scissors
aluminum foil
utility gloves
1 block of dry ice
34-quart (32-liter)
    plastic tub
empty cereal box
marker
flashlight
warm water

Step 1: Clear out a corner of the living room. Have an adult attach white bedsheets to the ceiling with thumbtacks or masking tape. The sheets should hang in front of the corner.

Step 2: To create ghosts, paint scary faces on white paper plates using glow-in-the-dark paint. Tape the plates to the bedsheets with masking tape.

Step 3: Pull apart cheesecloth to look like spiderwebs. Have an adult attach the cheesecloth to the ceiling with thumbtacks or masking tape. The cheesecloth should fall in front of the bedsheet. Arrange the cheesecloth so the scary faces are visible.

Step 4: Cut pieces of aluminum foil into long strips. Roll up each strip. Twist the ends of the first piece together to secure. Then insert the second piece through the first piece and twist the ends together. Continue with each piece until you have a long chain. Drape the chain in the cheesecloth.

Step 5: Have an adult place the block of dry ice in the plastic tub using utility gloves. Set the tub behind the cheesecloth.

Step 6: Cut apart a cereal box. Draw a pair of scary eyes on one of the large panels. Cut out the eyes with scissors.

Step 7: Hide yourself behind a chair or couch across the room from the sheet. Shine the flashlight through the cardboard with the scary eyes. Project the eyes onto the bedsheet.

Step 8: Right before your guests arrive, have an adult pour warm water into the tub. The dry ice will start to smoke. As the water cools, the smoke will lessen. Add more warm water to create more smoke.

TIP

Record your own scary sounds to play for your friends. Clank metal silverware together to sound like rattling chains. Blow and whistle to make stormy sounds. Use your own voice to make ghostly noises.

Witch's Kitchen

Turn your kitchen into a witch's cottage filled with wicked goodies. Create a cauldron filled with eyeballs. Turn a pumpkin and vegetables into one of the witch's unlucky victims. Invite your friends to eat him!

WHAT YOU NEED:

1 small pumpkin
pumpkin carving scraping tool
pumpkin carving saw tool
3 or 4 yards (3 or 4 meters) black tulle
scissors
plastic wrap
small plate
vegetables, washed and cut
spoon
ranch-flavored dip
crackers
2 small bowls
gummy worms
candy corn
markers
gray construction paper

TIP

Use small white or orange pumpkin gourds to hold candy. Ask an adult to cut off the tops of the gourds. Clean out the insides and pour in the candy.

Step 1: Ask an adult to help you gut and carve a pumpkin. Be sure to remove all the guts. Scrape the walls clean with the scraping tool. Then cut out two eyes and a wide mouth with the saw tool.

Step 2: Cover the countertops with black **tulle**. Cut into pieces to fit if needed.

Step 3: Set the pumpkin on top of the tulle. Spread a long piece of plastic wrap in front of the pumpkin. You'll create the pumpkin's "body" on the plastic. Set a small plate in front of the pumpkin's mouth.

Step 4: Use the fresh vegetables to create the pumpkin's arms and legs.

Step 5: Scoop some dip into the pumpkin's mouth. Put the rest of the dip onto the plate. The pumpkin should look as if it is throwing up. Arrange crackers around the dip.

Step 6: Fill small bowls with gummy worms and candy corn. Set on the countertops.

Step 7: Use markers and construction paper to label the candy as "Earwax" and "Rotting Worms." Fold the signs in half and set them in front of the bowls.

tulle—a sheer, often stiffened silk, rayon, or nylon netting used mainly for veils or ballet costumes

27

Zombieland

Your friends may have survived your haunted house, but they still need to walk through the backyard. Make funny or scary tombstones out of cardboard. Then have a few friends dress up like zombies to stalk the graveyard—and your guests!

WHAT YOU NEED:

pencil
several large pieces
  of cardboard
scissors
old newspaper
gray spray paint
black permanent marker
paintbrush
white glow-in-the-dark
  acrylic paint
wooden paint stir sticks
duct tape
dirt and/or old leaves
old gardening gloves
old shoes or boots

YOUR NAME HERE

REST IN PIECES

Step 1: Using a pencil, draw several tombstone shapes on cardboard pieces. Cut out with a scissors.

Step 2: Take the tombstones outside. Set the tombstones on old newspaper and spray paint them. Be sure to follow the instructions and safety precautions on the spray paint can. Let dry.

Step 3: Using a marker, write funny or spooky statements on the tombstones. Some ideas include "Rest in Pieces," "Deposits Only," and "Your Name Here." Paint over the words with glow-in-the-dark paint. Let dry.

Step 4: Tape one wooden paint stir stick to the back of each tombstone with duct tape.

Step 5: Stick the tombstones in the ground. Place piles of dirt or leaves in front of each tombstone.

Step 6: Stuff old gloves with newspaper. Place the gloves and shoes in the piles so they look like they are sticking out of the graves.

Step 7 (not pictured): Ask some friends to dress up like zombies. Have them walk slowly around the tombstones. If your tombstones are large enough, zombies can jump out from behind them when people walk by.

TIP

Have an adult buy spray paint that dries to look like real stone. Your tombstones will be even spookier!

Glossary

cauldron (KAWL-druhn)—a large kettle, often associated with witches' brews

gourd (GORD)—a small fruit with a shape similar to that of a squash or pumpkin

silhouette (sil-oo-ET)—an outline of something that shows its shape

sinister (SIN-uh-stur)—seeming evil and threatening

tulle (TOOL)—a sheer, often stiffened silk, rayon, or nylon netting used mainly for veils or ballet costumes

Read More

Aloian, Molly. *Halloween*. Celebrations in My World. New York: Crabtree Pub. Company, 2009.

Ipcizade, Catherine. *How to Make Frightening Halloween Decorations*. Halloween Extreme. Mankato, Minn.: Capstone Press, 2011.

Llimós, Anna. *Haunted House Adventure Crafts*. Fun Adventure Crafts. Berkeley Heights, N.J.: Enslow Publishers, 2010.

Old, Wendie. *The Halloween Book of Facts and Fun*. Morton Grove, Ill.: Albert Whitman & Co., 2007.

Internet Sites

FactHound offers a safe, fun way to find Internet sites related to this book. All of the sites on FactHound have been researched by our staff.

Here's all you do:

Visit *www.facthound.com*

Type in this code: 9781429654210

Check out projects, games and lots more at
www.capstonekids.com

Index